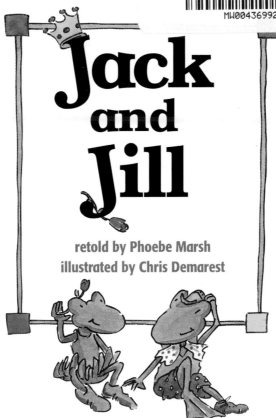

Jack and Jill

retold by Phoebe Marsh
illustrated by Chris Demarest

Scott Foresman

Editorial Offices: Glenview, Illinois • New York, New York
Sales Offices: Reading, Massachusetts • Duluth, Georgia
Glenview, Illinois • Carrollton, Texas • Menlo Park, California

Jack and Jill went up the hill…

to get a pail of water.

Jack fell down.

He broke his crown.

And Jill came tumbling after.

What does Jack do?

What does Jill do?

They have fun!